The GRUMPY GUIDE *to* LIFE

OBSERVATIONS *by* GRUMPY CAT

CHRONICLE BOOKS

SAN FRANCISCO

 *Thanks to:*

Bryan, **Tabatha**, **Chyrstal**, and **Elizabeth Bundesen**, **Ben Lashes**, **Kia Kamran**, **Michael Morris**, **Wynn Rankin**, **Michelle Clair**, **Lia Brown**, **April Whitney**, **Albee Dalbotten**, **Al Hassas**, **Julianne Freund**, **Mike Adkins**, **Heather Taylor**, **Emilie Sandoz**, **Pokey**, **Shaggy**, and **Grumpy's Frienemies** everywhere!

Library of Congress Cataloging-in-Publication
Data is available.

ISBN: 978-1-4521-3423-9

Manufactured in China

Designed by Michael Morris

10 9 8 7 6 5 4 3 2 1

Chronicle Books LLC
680 Second Street
San Francisco, California 94107
www.chroniclebooks.com

Contents

A Word from

GRUMPY CAT

We all need advice from time to time.

WELL, *YOU* DO.

I'm perfect just the way I am, which is why you're looking for my advice in the first place.

This book is full of thoughts and lessons gathered through a life of grumpiness.

If it shows just one person how to be miserable and grumpy and ensures that person never tries to talk to me again, it will have been worth it.

How do you use this book?
You look like you probably
need things spelled out for
you pretty clearly.
Let me make it easy for you:

1: UNDERSTAND YOU NEED HELP FROM AN EXPERT (ME).

2: CONTINUE TURNING THE PAGES OF THIS BOOK.

3: FOLLOW MY ADVICE.

4: REPEAT.

Got it?
Wait, don't tell me.
I honestly don't care.

IF AT FIRST YOU DON'T SUCCEED

GOOD

FAILURE
~~Success~~

The truth is, it's much easier to fail than it is to succeed. Why not just sit back and coast all the way to mediocrity? It's that or never-ending toil toward a meaningless goal. The choice is yours.

BELIEVE YOU CAN'T
AND YOU'RE
HALFWAY THERE.

KNOW WHEN TO QUIT:
before you even get started.

Practice **NEGATIVE** thinking.

NEVER LEAD. Always follow.
It's easier to trip someone
from behind.

IF LIFE DEALS YOU LEMONS,

THROW THEM
AT SOMEONE.

SOMETHING BETTER COULD BE JUST AROUND THE CORNER.
That's why I prefer to move as little as possible.

The only thing better than doing something yourself
IS TRICKING SOMEONE INTO DOING IT FOR YOU.

SUCCESS IS JUST FAILURE WAITING TO HAPPEN.

Encourage others to keep
trying even when hope
is lost. It's not that they'll
succeed in the end,
**BUT IT SURE IS
FUN TO WATCH
THEM STRUGGLE.**

DON'T TAKE "YES" FOR AN ANSWER.

LIVE YOUR DREAM,

but only if that dream is to ruin everyone else's dreams.

Set the bar low.
Then just sit back and
WATCH PEOPLE TRIP ON IT.

QUIT WHILE YOU'RE AHEAD.
Quit while you're behind.
The important thing to remember is this:
QUIT.

ALWAYS SAY NEVER.

Don't be afraid to break a few eggs.
**PREFERABLY ON
SOMEONE'S HEAD.**

IT'S IMPORTANT TO MAKE MISTAKES.

Make enough of them, and you'll be asked to stop working entirely.

It's not whether you win or lose—
**IT'S HOW YOU REFUSE
TO PARTICIPATE.**

SUCCESSFUL PEOPLE
know what they want and go for it.

GRUMPY PEOPLE lock the door
after they leave and take all their stuff.

**WHO'S THE SUCCESSFUL
ONE NOW?**

When opportunity knocks,
BOLT THE DOOR.

Love and Friendship

It's impossible to avoid having relationships with others. Trust me, I've tried. Certain people will always attach themselves to you and refuse to let go. That doesn't mean you have to start being friendly or submitting to hugs. There are plenty of ways to deal with the people that won't leave you alone. You might even get lucky and make them grumpy in the process.

A GOOD FRIEND
ALWAYS LISTENS.

Which is as good a reason as any to
never listen to anyone. Ever.
(You don't want people to get
the wrong idea.)

Being an enemy means
hating someone,
NO MATTER WHAT.

**NEVER BE AFRAID TO
IGNORE SOMEONE.**

You never know when you might
make a new enemy.

It's important to have alone time.
CONSTANTLY.

Remember this handy tip whenever someone starts talking to you:

STOP,

DROP,

AND ROLL YOUR EYES.

**GOOD FRIENDS KNOW
WHEN TO KEEP QUIET.**

GREAT FRIENDS DON'T TALK AT ALL.

MAKE OTHER PEOPLE'S BUSINESS YOUR BUSINESS.

How else will they know that you're right and they're wrong?

IT'S ALWAYS GOOD TO HAVE A PARTNER IN CRIME.

You need someone to blame when people start asking questions.

*Simple rules
for friendship:*

**IF ANYONE
TRIES TO GIVE
YOU ADVICE,
IGNORE THEM.**

**IF ANYONE
TRIES TO
IGNORE YOU,
GIVE THEM
ADVICE.**

Don't be afraid to tell someone
how you really feel.
**BONUS POINTS IF
THEY START CRYING.**

KEEP YOUR ENEMIES CLOSE.

THAT WAY YOU CAN'T SEE YOUR FRIENDS.

**A FRIEND IN NEED
IS A FRIEND INDEED.**

So just avoid making eye contact
with anyone, because helping people
is exhausting.

**YOUR HEART IS LIKE
A GARDEN.**

Tear up all the flowers and salt the earth
so that nothing can grow there ever again.

IMITATION IS THE BEST FORM OF BEING ANNOYING.

STRANGERS ARE JUST ENEMIES YOU HAVEN'T MET YET.

NO ONE EVER TRIES
TO HUG YOU WHEN
YOU'RE A CACTUS.

How did they get so lucky?

When's the last time you did something for others?

CORRECT ANSWER:

NEVER.

PEOPLE ARE LIKE
BALLS OF YARN.

For the most part they're boring and
useless, but I still get a lot of pleasure
out of watching them unravel.

NEXT TIME YOU THINK YOU'VE HIT BOTTOM, GIVE ME A CALL.

I'll hand you a shovel so you can keep going.

FROWN AND THE WHOLE WORLD FROWNS WITH YOU.

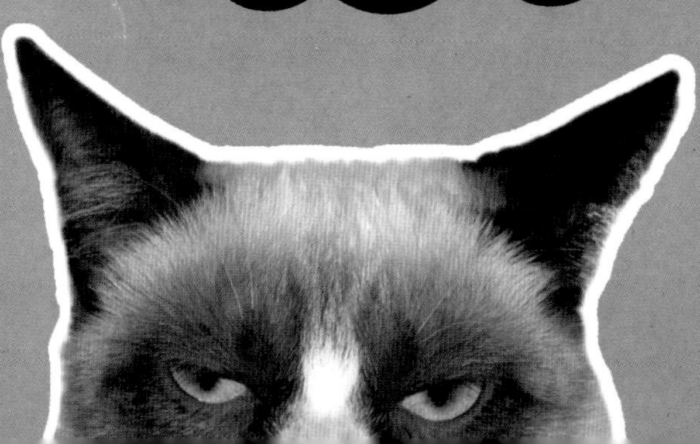

**STOP BEFORE YOU DO
SOMETHING I'LL REGRET.**

THE BEST THINGS
IN LIFE ARE

ANNOYING

The Inner Grump

Finally, something I actually care about: Myself. Being selfish is the best thing you can do for yourself. Literally. This section is full of tips to help you tune out the world and focus on yourself for a while. At the very least, it's a good excuse to not talk to anyone for a few days.

WHEN WRITING YOUR OWN LIFE STORY, BE THE VILLAIN.

FIND HAPPINESS
IN THE LITTLE THINGS.
The smaller they are, the easier it will be to fit them in the trash.

**EVERYONE HAS
A CONSCIENCE.**
It's best to find it and get that
thing under control before it keeps
you from doing anything I tell
you to do.

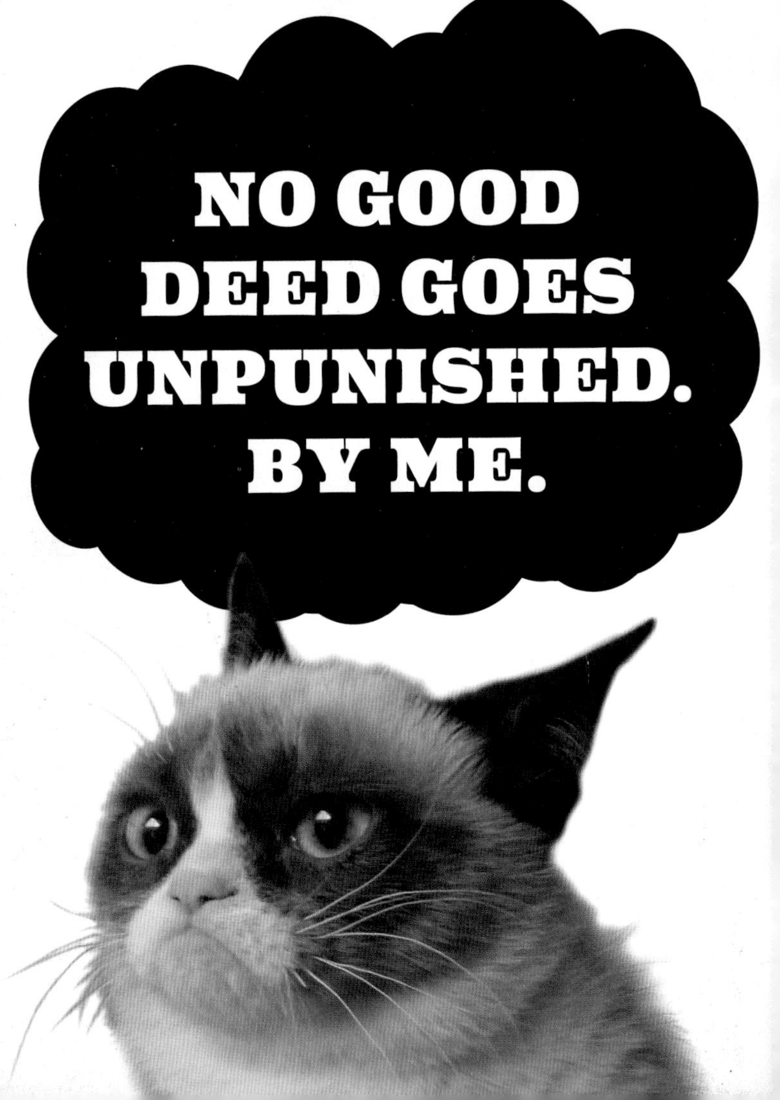
NO GOOD DEED GOES UNPUNISHED.
BY ME.

Contemplate life's big questions:

HOW DO I CONVINCE THE DOG TO RUN AWAY?

CAN I CHANGE THE LOCKS BEFORE EVERYONE GETS HOME?

WHOSE BIRTHDAY PARTY SHOULD I RUIN NEXT?

**THE JOURNEY IS
THE DESTINATION.**

So get out of here and don't
stop until you get there.

WHAT GOES UP
MUST COME DOWN.

So why bother with the up part?

ALL GOOD THINGS MUST
COME TO AN END.

That's why I suggest that you do us
all a favor and hurry them along.

TRYING NEW THINGS

IS A RECIPE FOR

DISAPPOINTMENT.

WHY PUT OFF UNTIL
TOMORROW WHAT YOU
CAN DO NEVER?

MAKE EVERY WAY

THE WRONG WAY

IT TAKES MORE ENERGY TO FROWN THAN TO SMILE.

That's more than enough exercise for the day.

When things are looking bright, **TRY CLOSING THE BLINDS.**

ASK YOURSELF THIS:
If a tree falls in the woods, does it still annoy me? And could I convince someone to stand near it before it happens?

PRACTICE

It's important to always
have a **CAN'T-DO** attitude.

Lies will set you free
**FROM HAVING TO TELL
THE TRUTH.**

LOOK AT THINGS FROM A DIFFERENT PERSPECTIVE.

My favorite one is "with my eyes closed."

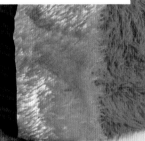

DEAD ENDS ARE A GREAT EXCUSE TO GIVE UP.

DON'T FORGET:

Every silver lining is part of a larger, darker cloud.

KEEP YOUR CHIN UP.

And the corners of your mouth down.

READING IS LIKE WATCHING TV,

except it's excruciatingly slow and
mind-numbingly boring.

TO BE OR
NOT TO BE.
I THINK YOU
KNOW MY
PREFERENCE.

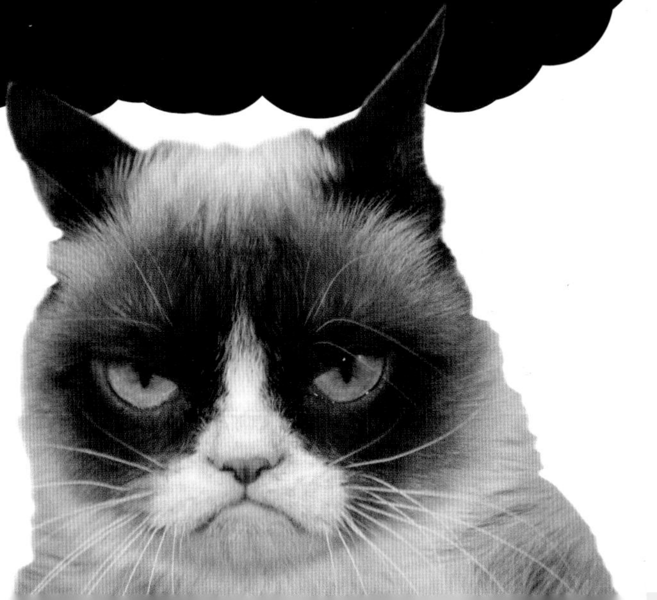

Home and Family

They say that home is where the heart is, but what if you don't have a heart? Well, you still need to live somewhere, so you might as well use it as an excuse to make everyone you live with as miserable as possible. Whether you call that place "home" or "a living nightmare," it's a place where you can let your grumpy self really come through.

TRY TO KEEP

ON TOP OF

THE HOUSEWORK.

IT'S IMPORTANT TO BE FLEXIBLE.

It makes it easier to hide from people that are looking for you.

Having a sibling around is like being forced to constantly look in a mirror at an inferior version of yourself.

WE DON'T CHOOSE OUR FAMILIES.

But we can choose to swipe at them if they get too close.

YOUR HOME IS YOUR CASTLE.

Which is why I recommend as many booby traps and well-placed vats of burning hot oil as possible.

It's true what they say:
You can never go home again.
**BECAUSE I CHANGED
THE LOCKS.**

Celebrating the holidays with your family **IS A GOOD WAY TO MAKE SURE NO ONE HAS A GOOD TIME.**

Memories warm the heart.
**ESPECIALLY WHEN THEY'RE
USED AS KINDLING.**

Family comes first.
**IN THE LIST OF THINGS
TO AVOID WHENEVER
POSSIBLE.**

THE BEST VACATIONS

are the ones you tell your family
about only after you've left.

LET SLEEPING DOGS LIE.
Otherwise they'll wake up and try to cuddle with you and that's just terrible.

**THERE IS NO RIGHT SIDE OF
BED TO WAKE UP ON,
SO DON'T EVEN TRY.**

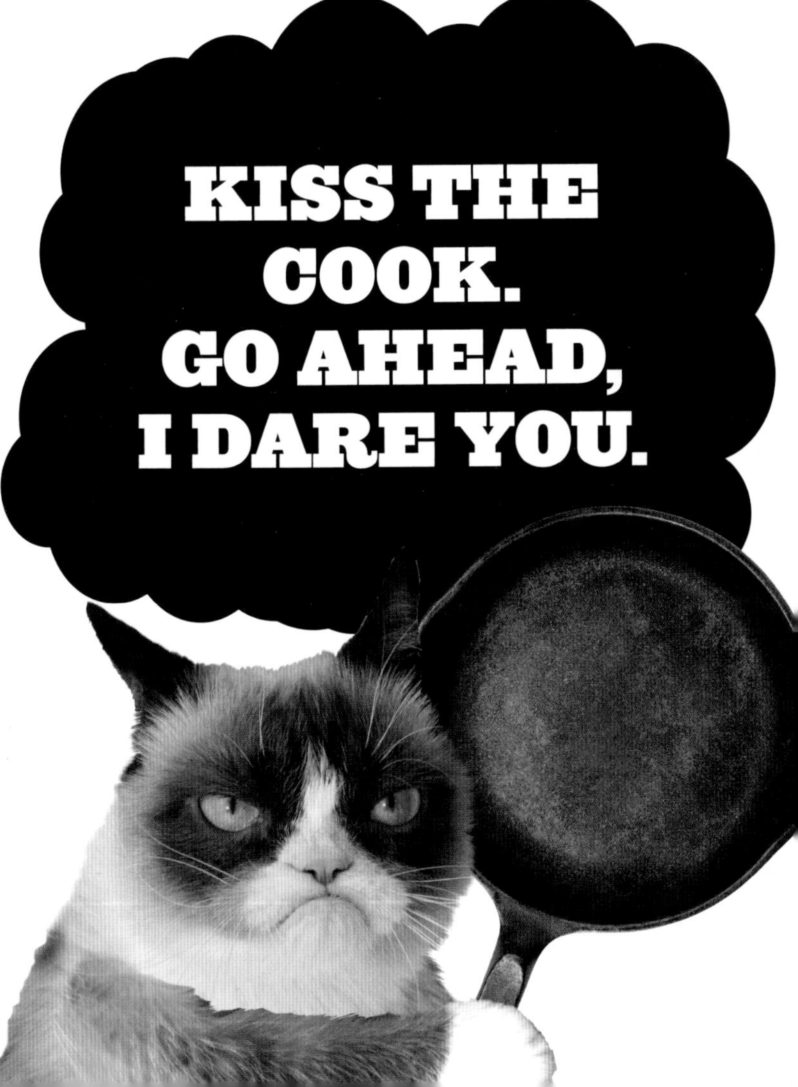
KISS THE COOK.
GO AHEAD,
I DARE YOU.

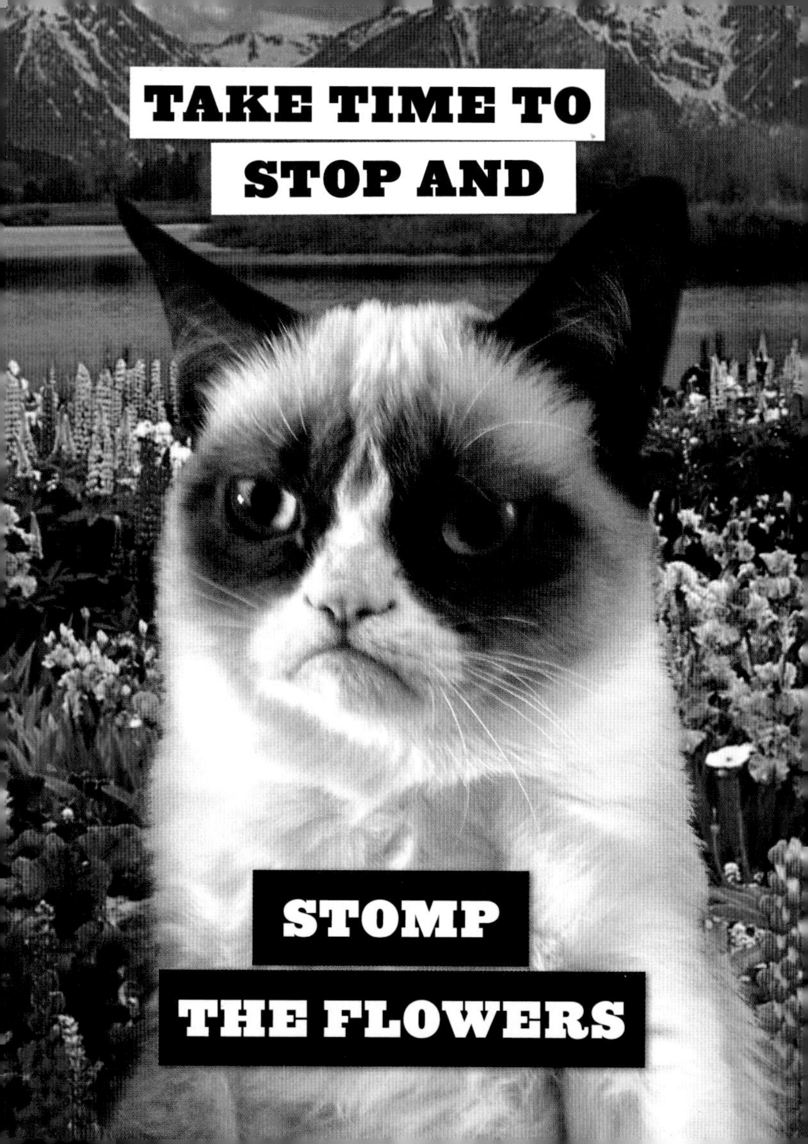
TAKE TIME TO
STOP AND
STOMP
THE FLOWERS

Nature

A glorious sunrise, a majestic snow-capped mountain range, a quiet forest—there are so many reasons to hate nature. You say, "warm summer nights and fields of wildflowers." I say "swarms of mosquitoes and terrible allergies." Don't let Mother Nature trick you into thinking she's your friend. She's out to get you, just like everyone else.

**WHEN YOU'RE LOOKING
UP AT THE STARS,
REMEMBER THIS:**

They're probably dead and you
just don't know it yet.

THE TIDE IS A GREAT REMINDER

that whatever you do doesn't really matter because it will just get washed away and forgotten.

THE GRASS IS
ALWAYS GREENER

where you don't have to share
it with anyone else.

Being out in nature
always reminds me of
**HOW SMALL AND
INSIGNIFICANT YOU ARE.**

IF YOU SEE A
BEAUTIFUL RAINBOW,

take comfort in the fact that someone
somewhere is getting rained on. Maybe
even getting struck by lightning.

THE GREAT THING ABOUT THE OUTDOORS

is that you can walk around for days and not see anyone.

SNOW IS NATURE'S WAY OF SAYING,

"go back inside and get in bed, you idiot."

DON'T BE AFRAID TO GO OUT ON A LIMB.

How else will you be able to drop things on people's heads when they try to rescue you?

**THERE ARE PLENTY
OF FISH IN THE SEA.**

Annoying, ugly, smelly fish.

Finding yourself between a rock and a hard place is just fine,

ESPECIALLY WHEN YOU'RE HIDING FROM SOMEONE YOU CAN'T STAND.

FLOWERS ARE JUST NATURE SHOWING OFF.

We get it, nature. *You have colors.*
You don't need to rub our faces in it.

NEXT TIME YOU'RE FEELING PRETTY GOOD ABOUT HOW THINGS ARE GOING IN YOUR LIFE,

remember that the dinosaurs were probably feeling that way, too, before that meteor fell.

FALL IS MY FAVORITE SEASON.

Wait, no, I got that wrong. It's my favorite thing to watch people do.

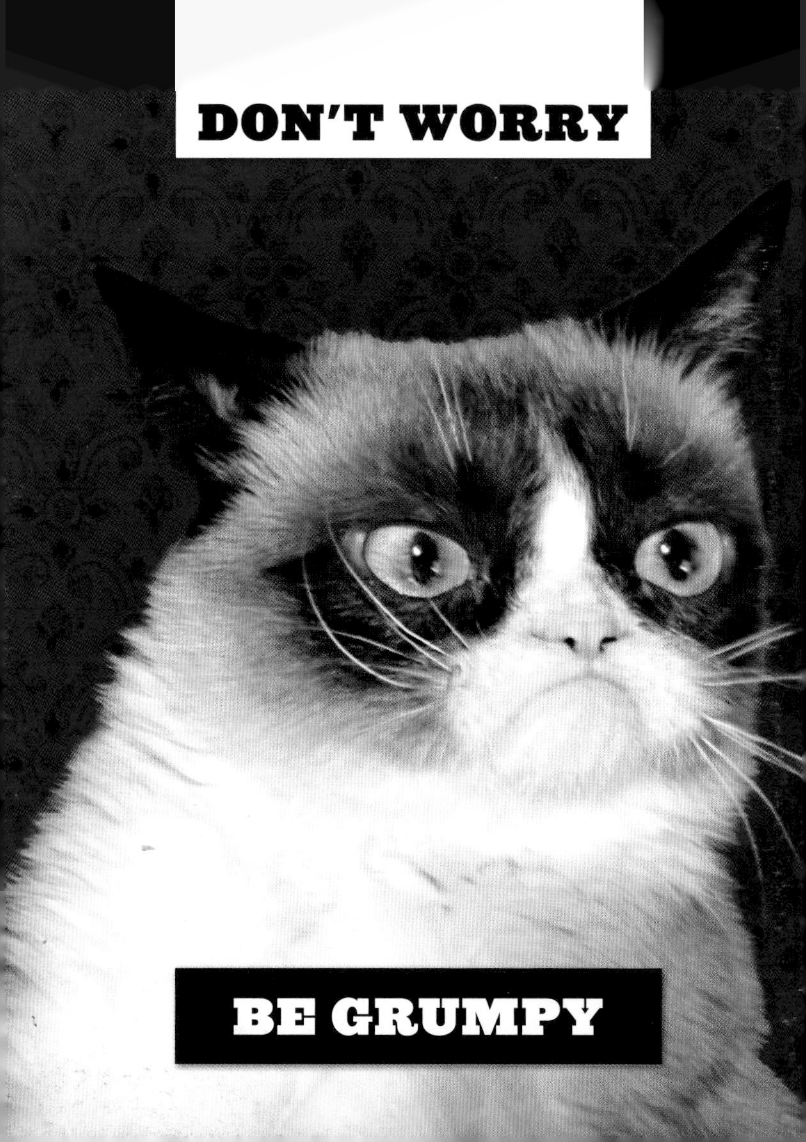
DON'T WORRY
BE GRUMPY

Happiness

This page left intentionally blank.